STOCKING STUFFERS FOR MEN: CHRISTMAS GIFT:

EXERCISE YOUR MIND & KEEP YOUR BRAIN Y(

Mens Stocking Stuffer Ideas & Christmas Gifts for Adults T

TABLE OF CONTENTS

Crossword Explanation

This book contains 25 symmetrical word search puzzles. Each puzzle is made up of a 15X15 grid with a symmetrical layout of black squares. An example of an empty puzzle can be seen below.

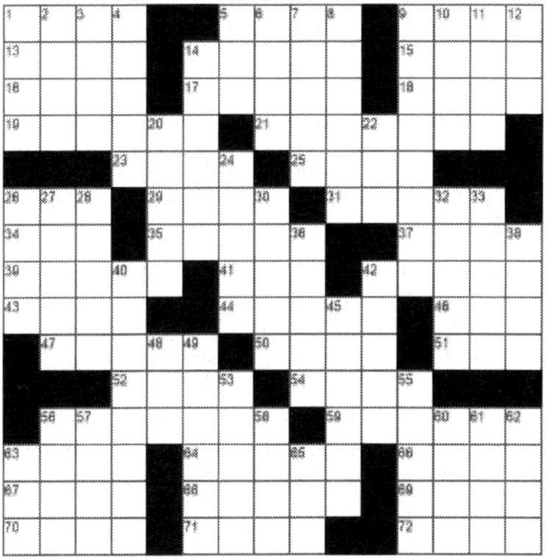

A list of clues is provided below each puzzle. Each clue corresponds to a certain location on the puzzle. Once you figure out the clue, then fill in the corresponding squares in the puzzle. Continue to do this until you have the entire puzzle filled in.

Good Luck and Merry Christmas!

Puzzle #1

ACROSS

1 Disconnected
4 City
9 Card suit
14 Legume
15 Sign of the zodiac
16 Compelled to go
17 Moray
18 Large wave
19 Great ape
20 Chowder ingredient
22 Make a choice
24 Pigpen
25 Expression
27 Chick holder
29 Computer equipment
32 Recites numbers
35 Box
36 Monkey's cousin
38 Colored People's association
40 Dimension
42 Appoints
44 Telegram
45 Clean thoroughly
47 Gap
49 Lick
50 Catch in a net
52 "Only one substance" belief
54 __ Lanka
55 Constellation
56 Bard's before
59 Removed
63 Ca. University
67 Terra __ (type of clay)
69 Radiuses
71 Roman three
72 Go after
73 Clerk
74 Decade
75 Leaves out
76 Forehead covering
77 Time zone

DOWN

1 Organization of Petroleum Exporting Countries
2 Touch
3 Syllables used in songs (2 wds.)
4 Entrance rug
5 Male Ireland dwellers
6 Helper
7 Cereal
8 Island
9 Front passenger seat's name
10 Golfer's goal
11 Alack's partner
12 Indent
13 Fidgety
21 Wet dirt
23 Executive
26 Hair stuff
28 Chew
29 Chop
30 Purple vegetable
31 Big hit
32 Whipped dairy food
33 Animal end parts
34 Beat it!
35 Public transportation
37 Referee
39 High-school club
41 "Calciums" antacid brand
43 Rebuking
46 Looks over the book, again
48 Vane direction
51 Mr.
53 Note of debt
56 Repeat
57 Part of a house
58 Decorative needle case
60 Arabian
61 Soap Opera
62 Paradise
64 Quote
65 Untruths
66 Am not
68 Explosive
70 __ A Small World...

Puzzle #2

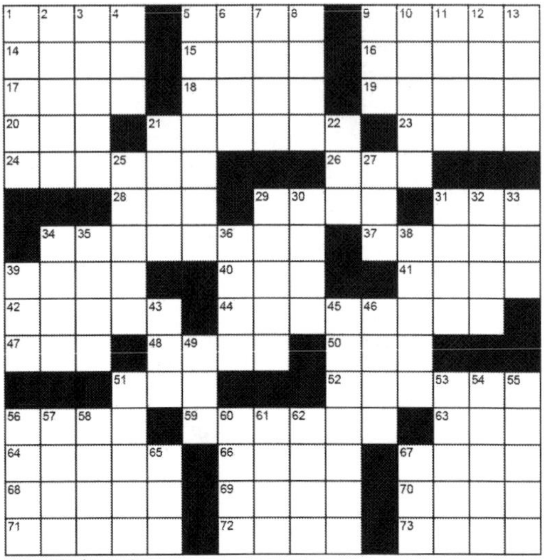

www.CrosswordWeaver.com

ACROSS

1 No longer for sale
5 Cheats
9 Type of car
14 Region
15 Dinner bread
16 Adios
17 Myriad
18 Water (Sp.)
19 A piece of turf
20 Deli order
21 Perplexity
23 Machines that rotates on the ceiling
24 On the ship
26 Climbing vine
28 Central Intelligence Agency
29 Prefix for half
31 Poem
34 Something short lived
37 Empower
39 Accent mark
40 Pooch
41 Slime
42 Musical composition
44 Animal and vegetable eater
47 Mountain Time
48 Beats
50 Butane
51 Building addition
52 Relatives
56 Vertex
59 Soup legume
63 Card game
64 Wooden box
66 Rampage
67 Association (abbr.)
68 __ cotta (clay)
69 Stake
70 Criminal
71 What a dropped melon does
72 Origination
73 Potato sprouts

DOWN

1 Dance
2 Toothbrush brand
3 Musical "slow"
4 24 hours
5 Pontiac car type (2 wds.)
6 Bear or Berra
7 Socket's metal prongs
8 Bang down
9 Melancholy
10 Teach
11 Prima donna
12 Long time
13 Cashews, for example
21 Canal
22 Place
25 Was sore
27 Compete
29 Band instruments
30 Take in
31 Smell
32 Nap
33 Female sheep
34 Freudian selves
35 Move a boat by pole
36 Economics abrv.
38 Lasso
39 Extremity
43 Night bird
45 Lit
46 Famous ski resort
49 Peaked
51 More
53 Easy
54 Turn out
55 Musical pieces
56 Deeds
57 Preparation (abbr.)
58 Royalty
60 Time periods
61 Before ten
62 Carry
65 Sup
67 Snacked

Puzzle #3

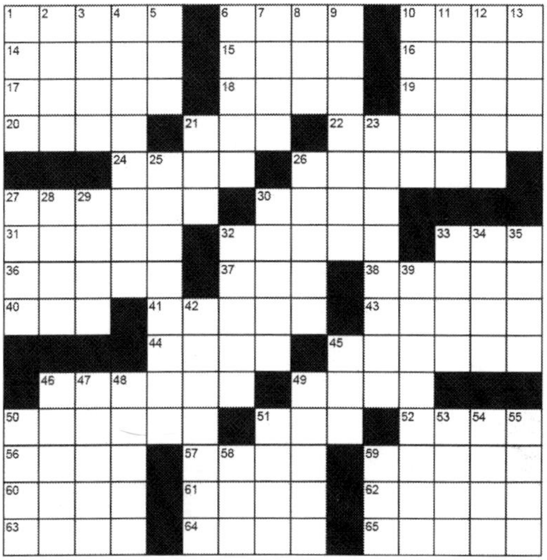

ACROSS

1 Sheer, triangular scarf
6 Rise (2 wds.)
10 Niche
14 Muslim's religion
15 __ Major (Big Dipper)
16 Bone
17 Slouch
18 Not hard
19 Skirt
20 Swarm
21 American sign language
22 Brand of frozen dough
24 Chances of winning
26 Anchored
27 Places at intervals
30 Pickle herb
31 Predatory bird
32 Not happily
33 Pen brand
36 Risen
37 Nervous system
38 Approximate date
40 Harden
41 Gone With the Wind's Mr. Butler
43 Colder
44 Melody
45 Horses
46 Overrun
49 Removes the water
50 Women, (slang)
51 Thai
52 Aura
56 Same
57 Computer "button"
59 Walnut's cousin
60 For fear that
61 Heroic
62 Souvenir
63 Belief
64 Discount
65 Composition

DOWN

1 Clenched hand
2 Island
3 Hint
4 Lazy summer beds
5 Referee
6 Gauge
7 Spoken
8 Ship initials
9 Employee wage list
10 Performer
11 Overly proper
12 Gorged
13 Flightless birds
21 Spots
23 Mecca (2 wds.)
25 Defected
26 In the middle of
27 Thick carpet
28 Cut the peel off
29 Truant
30 Author of "The Inferno"
32 Fragrance
33 Soft cheese
34 Chilled
35 Autos
39 Floe (2 wds.)
42 Brazen women
45 __ Lanka
46 Peeved
47 Sound
48 Soft drink brand
49 Twist
50 Indonesian island
51 Work
53 Organization concerned with civil liberties (abbr.)
54 Put down
55 One time
58 Accountant
59 Before (prefix)

Puzzle #4

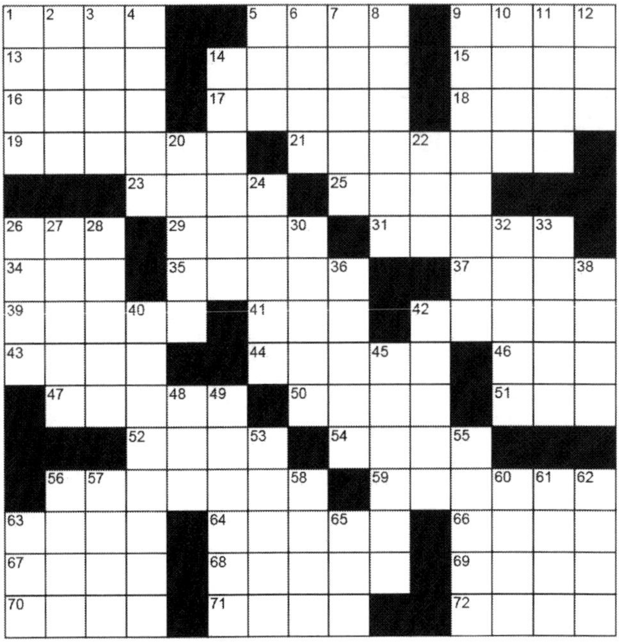

ACROSS

1 Small particle
5 Dog food brand
9 Top of the head
13 Presidents office
14 Bundle
15 Aegis
16 Left
17 Impressionist painter
18 Brash
19 Very soft fur
21 Former name for Benin
23 Faction
25 Naughty or __
26 Body of water
29 Alter
31 Jabs
34 Farm animal
35 Jacob's father
37 Leaf maker
39 Embellish
41 Cubic centimeter
42 Goatee
43 Meager
44 Leer
46 Cask
47 Radio detection and ranging
50 Hang-up
51 Before, poetically
52 Antiaircraft fire
54 Capital of the Ukraine
56 Venezuela capital
59 Rib joiners
63 Meat alternative
64 Type of shorts
66 Legible
67 Japanese dress
68 Mischievous
69 To
70 Draw
71 Has toed
72 Desist

DOWN

1 American state
2 Kiln
3 Zest
4 Singing parts
5 Expression of surprise
6 Allow to borrow
7 Eulogy
8 Hereof (2 wds.)
9 Spread through
10 Malaria
11 Straightened
12 Vane direction
14 Tastes of
20 Tree product
22 Fall mo.
24 Playing groups
26 Canned meat brand
27 Bedspread feather
28 Ancient Greek marketplace
30 Abides
32 Halt
33 Dried up
36 Clang
38 Brim
40 Apple (2 wds.)
42 Father
45 Cereal fruit
48 Wing
49 Noise
53 Painter Freida
55 Goddess
56 Fuel
57 Hairstyle
58 Unhurt
60 Let
61 Treaty organization
62 On top
63 Cooking measurement
65 Child

Puzzle #5

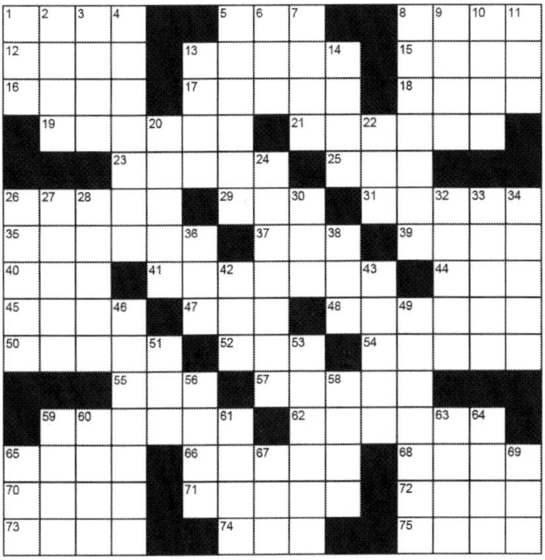

ACROSS

1 Cain's brother
5 Church bench
8 Colorless
12 Coat
13 Musical
15 Air (prefix)
16 Kid's cereal brand
17 European nation
18 Invent
19 O.T. prophet
21 Without difficulty
23 Rebound
25 Not (refix)
26 Association (abbr.)
29 Clip
31 Strike workers
35 __ Aries
37 Snatch
39 Belief
40 Music
41 Asphalt origin
44 Fall behind
45 Flow
47 Take to court
48 Godly
50 Used a keyboard
52 Gross national product (abbr.)
54 Tramps
55 Rio de Janeiro
57 Fiend
59 Booths
62 What the Tin Man needed
65 Bewitch
66 Speaks with a hoarse voice
68 Domain
70 __ upon a time
71 Birds "thumb"
72 Not any
73 Necklace part
74 Compass point
75 Double-reed instrument

DOWN

1 Clever
2 Stark
3 Wicked
4 Ancient language dictionary
5 Big snake
6 Epoch
7 Deception
8 Mona Lisa painter
9 Authentic
10 Navy's rival
11 Jazz
13 Prevaricator
14 Greenish-blue color
20 Leah's husband
22 Distress call
24 Subtrahend subtracted from this
26 Toward the rear of the ship
27 Gruff
28 Frame
30 Highest trump in some loo
32 Improvise a speech
33 Keno
34 Wise people
36 Sister for short
38 Bedroom furniture
42 Pull
43 Naught
46 Copied
49 Etna
51 Disrespect
53 Humans
56 Gumbo
58 Permission to enter a foreign country
59 Bull
60 Ancient Indian
61 Sold at a discount
63 Arabian
64 Roman emperor
65 Chore
67 Star
69 Popeye's yes

Puzzle #6

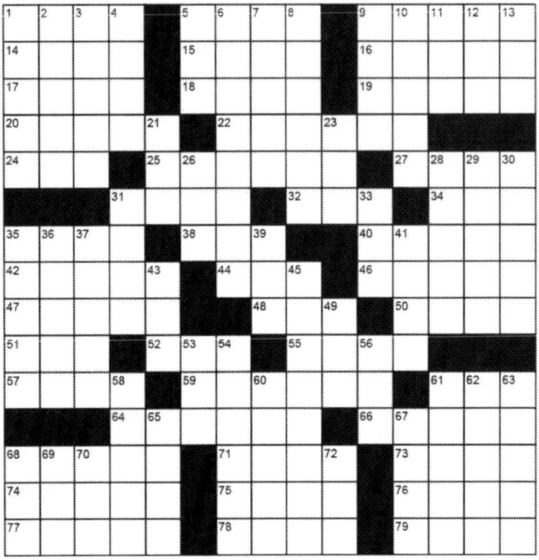

ACROSS

1 Top of the head
5 File
9 Operatic bass
14 Seaweed substance
15 Off-Broadway award
16 Nudge
17 Cab
18 Vigor
19 Use a divining rod
20 Tiny particle
22 Ending
24 Affirmation
25 Cyclic
27 Cleaning agent
31 Shank
32 Ball holder
34 Certified public accountant
35 Reserve Officers Training Corps.
38 Metric weight unit
40 Award
42 Constellation
44 Snack
46 Peel corn
47 Lessen
48 Lingerie
50 Mined metals
51 Directory (abbr.)
52 X
55 Institution (abbr.)
57 Prod
59 Holy places
61 Farm credit administration (abbr.)
64 Hawk
66 Teacher's writing tool
68 Remit (2 wds.)
71 Fredrick's nickname
73 Aroma
74 Sedimentary rock
75 Eye
76 Business note
77 Submissive
78 Milk product
79 Sports channel

DOWN

1 Easily taken advantage of
2 Open mouthed
3 Duties
4 Little Mermaid's love
5 Knock off
6 To remain
7 Fathers
8 Allow
9 Sleeping places
10 Lotion ingredients
11 South by west
12 Distress call
13 To be in debt
21 Rate
23 Frozen water
26 Masculine pronoun
28 Happen
29 Quickly
30 Leaves the car
31 Scotsman
33 Aurora
35 Routes
36 Circle
37 Jeweled headdress
39 Gossip
41 Ruined
43 Tulle
45 Trike
49 Colony insect
53 Clairvoyance
54 Linear
56 Pouch
58 Greek government
60 Horse noise
61 Disappears
62 Walk noisily
63 City in Ohio
65 Rushed
67 Where a family lives
68 Clock time
69 Expression of surprise
70 Thanksgiving vegetable
72 Opens lock

Puzzle #7

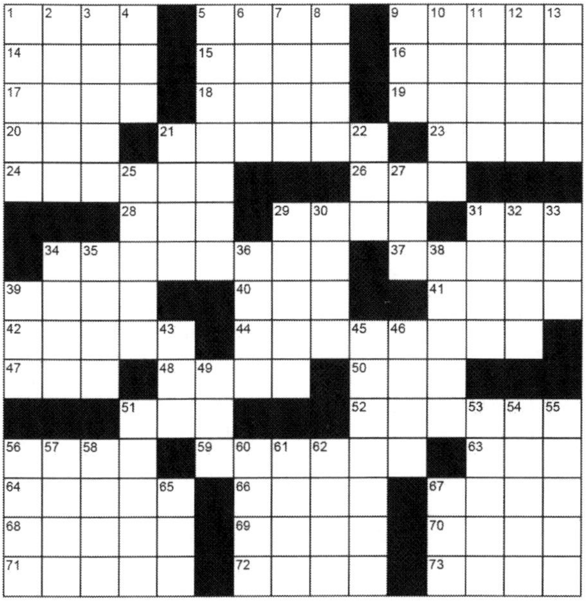

ACROSS

1 Jab
5 Star Trek Automoton's
9 Devour (2 wds.)
14 Fetching
15 Jewish calendar month
16 Tilt
17 Lotion ingredient
18 Uh-uh
19 Support
20 Zilch
21 One who dies for a cause
23 Former W. German capital
24 Internal organ
26 Three
28 Constrictor
29 Present
31 Resort hotel
34 Lethargically
37 Eyed
39 Presence
40 Not very light
41 Acorns
42 Pleads
44 Eats Meat and Vegitation
47 Skirt edge
48 Simply
50 Mayan
51 Pounds per square inch
52 Pecan (2 wds.)
56 Tiny spider
59 Type of snake
63 Roberto's yes
64 Rub out
66 Courts
67 Costa __
68 Anglo-__
69 Manage
70 Wields
71 Flavoring
72 Brews
73 Bare

DOWN

1 Looks over
2 Spring flower
3 Coral reef
4 Bumbling insect
5 Monkey companions
6 Scent
7 Absorbed
8 Color
9 Extra-sensory perception
10 Defense
11 Dorothy's dog
12 On top
13 Pennsylvania (abbr.)
21 Cat's cry
22 River (Spanish)
25 Type of wood
27 The other half of Jima
29 Slippery
30 ___ book, church music
31 Mumble
32 Peter, for short
33 Advertisements
34 Desperate
35 Stack of paper
36 Teen hero
38 Dwarf
39 Miles per hour
43 Morse Code
45 Exacts
46 Of no value
49 Clip
51 Spanish coins
53 Twang
54 Stomache sore
55 Kid
56 Plateau
57 Asian country
58 Ride on the runway
60 Young Women's Christian Association
61 Adze
62 Expect
65 Vane direction
67 Booze

Puzzle #8

ACROSS

1 Fern seed
6 Root vegetable
9 Wind pointer
13 Water movers
14 Stage of life
15 __ up (hiding)
16 Sugar-free brand
17 Remind
18 Oscar
19 Sour
20 Tan colors
22 Chinese sauce
23 Rapid eye movement
24 Stood opposite
25 Musical symbol
27 Quoth
29 Forever
33 Rumpus
34 North American nation
35 Ancien German character
36 Rusk
39 Cycles per second
40 Indian horse
41 Supplication
42 Pop (plr.)
43 Biddy
44 Mid semester test
46 Jargon
49 Lake
50 Flightless bird
51 Had been
53 Cold
56 Giant's wife
58 __ matter
59 Drench
61 Gone to lunch
62 Longitudinal
63 Contrapuntal ompositional technique
64 Lode yield
65 Smooth tightly twisted thread
66 52 weeks
67 Neither's partner
68 Cinder

DOWN

1 Pointed weapon
2 Sign of the zodiac
3 Type of American Express card
4 Marsh plant
5 East southeast
6 Boat
7 Water (Spanish)
8 Humility
9 Wedding promise
10 Alack's partner
11 Roman emperor
12 Whirl
15 "__ makes waste"
20 Genghis __
21 Small particle
24 Mix
26 Making mistakes
28 Imagine
30 Sister
31 Picnic pest
32 MGM's Lion
34 Delivery service
36 Words per minute
37 Boxer Muhammad
38 ___ up
39 African nation
40 South American country
42 Snob
43 Pork servings
45 Wear away
47 Like an owl
48 "Hot __"
50 Organic compound
52 Profits
53 Flukey
54 Indication
55 Meditation
57 European monetary unit
58 Center of rotation
60 Possessive pronoun
62 Wing

Puzzle #9

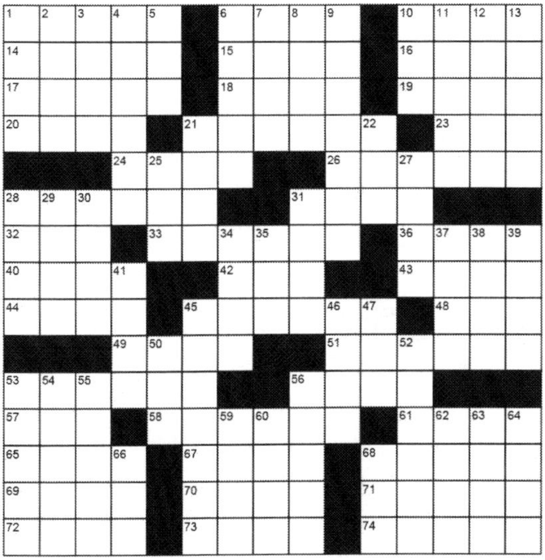

ACROSS

1 Short poem
6 Captain (abbr.)
10 Convexity
14 Inspect
15 Super Man
16 Ride the waves
17 Scarf
18 Press
19 Louvre
20 Receive votes
21 Bungle (2 wds.)
23 Adam's wife
24 Decorative needle case
26 Sponsored child
28 Fire starter
31 Sailors "hey"
32 Elver
33 Secretary
36 Flat
40 Slash
42 American Cancer Society (abbr.)
43 Cache
44 Tub spread
45 Fashionable
48 Bro. or sis.
49 Occupy
51 Baby's toy
53 National capital
56 Use a keyboard
57 Alien's spaceship
58 Beginnings
61 Black
65 Not yours
67 Cook quickly
68 Saw logs
69 Grand __
70 Meager
71 Fire residue
72 Cult
73 Killed
74 Greek sandwiches

DOWN

1 Fastener
2 Car
3 False god graven image
4 Type of whale
5 North American Indian
6 Texas stew
7 Air (prefix)
8 Bow
9 This evening
10 United States Ship (abbr.)
11 Beasts of burden
12 Well done!
13 Many times
21 Raise one's spirits
22 Also
25 Dynamite
27 Colors
28 Sego lily's bulb
29 Duck
30 Otherwise
31 Association (abbr.)
34 Where children can play
35 Sorbet
37 Large
38 Wicked
39 Northeast by east
41 Elias ___, sewing machine
45 Clichés
46 Towel
47 Talk incessantly
50 Ball
52 Teeny
53 Childhood disease
54 Ablaze
55 Audible
56 Hove
59 Rotate
60 Weed in a wheat field
62 Danish physicist
63 Dunking cookies
64 Loch __ monster
66 Extension (abbr.)
68 Swag

Puzzle #10

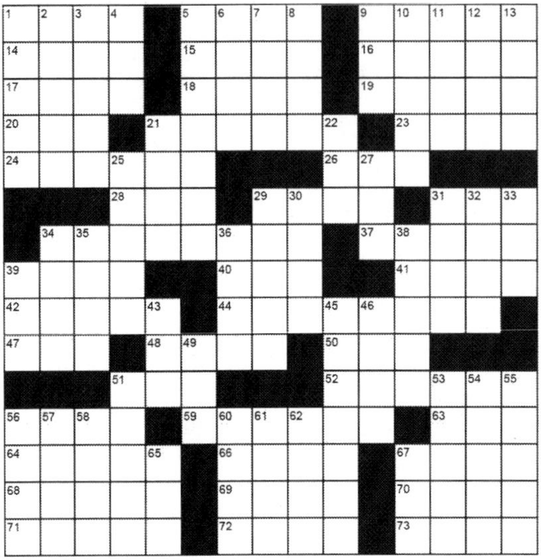

ACROSS

1 Brood
5 Apex
9 Hurray!
14 Capital of Peru
15 Stow
16 Type of gun
17 Do what you're told
18 Hand outs
19 Cut of beef
20 Can metal
21 House cat
23 Ceases
24 Played (2 wds.)
26 White-tailed sea eagle
28 Artist's creation
29 Soap Opera
31 Hotel
34 Capital of Wyoming
37 Asian nation
39 Actor Alda
40 Yours and mine
41 Chocolate and peppermint candy
42 Italian "dollars"
44 Rejecting
47 Beats per minute
48 Stink
50 Conger
51 Not max
52 Putting down
56 Qualified
59 Delight
63 Equal
64 Life form
66 Retired persons association (abbr.)
67 Messenger
68 Stop
69 Parent teacher groups
70 Beers
71 Small herring
72 Alleviate
73 Greek stringed instrument

DOWN

1 Indolence
2 Shinbone
3 Make corrections to
4 Path
5 Cooked until chewy (2 wds.)
6 Peachy
7 French Sudan
8 Adam's garden
9 Bacon-lettuce-tomato sandwich
10 Hot sandwich
11 Competition at the Greek games
12 Peddle
13 Iron
21 Anger
22 Electroencephalograph (abbr.)
25 Matador's passes at bull
27 Manned
29 Moved furtively
30 Short for aeronautical
31 Reel
32 Pain
33 Alternative (abbr.)
34 Barette
35 Lesion
36 Prow
38 Author Dickinson
39 Loose gown worn at mass
43 __ Lanka
45 Digress to former condition
46 Come close to
49 Compass point
51 Elite intellectuals' society
53 Pope's country
54 African country
55 Birds that make a gaggle
56 What children learn
57 Toot
58 Deceiver
60 Neck
61 Input
62 Extremely long time periods
65 Collect
67 Buddy

Puzzle #11

DOWN

1 Ran
2 Israel's son
3 Car rental agency
4 Corporate rule
5 Small bird
6 Spy
7 Healing plant
8 Singer Ronstadt
9 Record
10 Northeast by north
11 Bye
12 Chomper
13 Strict
21 Retail clothing store
22 Trickery
25 Popular president's initials
27 Blacken
28 Coupe
29 Blot
31 Knocks (2 wds.)
32 Hide away
34 Rope fiber
36 Capital of Western Samoa
38 Strange and frightening
39 Worship
40 Vegetable
41 Depend
46 Factual
47 Sports official
48 Every evening
52 Arbiter
54 Groggy
55 Deduce
56 Taboos
58 Cuss
60 Pondered
62 Skating area
64 International Natural Sciences Tournament (abbr.)
65 Oceans
66 Italian currency
67 Put down
68 Song by the Village People
70 African antelope

ACROSS

1 Excess flesh
5 Wee
10 Grabs
14 Tariff
15 Crippling disease
16 Alter
17 Demonic
18 With
19 Prick
20 Clashed
22 Smile scornfully
23 Fight
24 American Football Conference (abbr.)
26 Pot
27 Automobile
30 Cooking vessels
33 Morse code "T"
35 Hawaiian dancing
37 Green rinded fruit
42 A spinning toy (2 wds.)
43 Golfer's goal
44 Compose
45 Allergy medicine
49 Unpolluted
50 Fortify
51 One who inherits
53 Parent
54 Thief's hideout
57 United Parcel Service
59 Jewel
61 Dote
63 Hopefully
69 Member of an Arizona Indian tribe
70 Civet cat's cousin
71 Thailand
72 Engaging Connections Opportunities Networks (abbr.)
73 Whining voice type
74 Member of Cream
75 Writing table
76 Salaam
77 Father

Puzzle #12

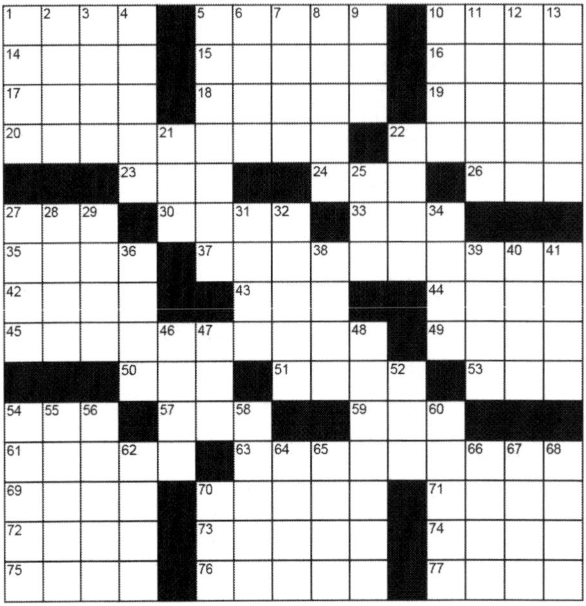

ACROSS

1 Excess flesh
5 Leading
10 Water carrier
14 Divide
15 Monkey's cousin
16 Fairy tale opener
17 Elide
18 Common people
19 Make a sweater
20 Sidled (3 wds.)
22 Hastening
23 Child
24 Observe secretly
26 Self
27 Genetic code
30 Possessive pronoun
33 Largest bird in Austrailia
35 Whorl
37 Boat navigation skill
42 Negative (prefix)
43 Take to court
44 Confident
45 Timber yeller
49 Stable gear
50 Male offspring
51 Decorative needle case
53 Concord e.g.
54 Clairvoyance
57 Fish eggs
59 Sward
61 Get up
63 Occurring at night
69 Ripped up
70 Recruit
71 American state
72 Always
73 Smooth
74 Flat
75 Remake
76 Covered roof
77 Traveled by horse

DOWN

1 Package label
2 Fancy car
3 Tel __
4 Pepper plant
5 Refers indirectly
6 Pile
7 Discharge
8 Cars
9 Sere
10 Dawdling
11 Red headed orphan
12 Frosting
13 Drop (2 wds.)
21 Morse code "T"
22 Anthem
25 Pod vegetable
27 Depict
28 Taboo
29 Singing voice
31 Lay
32 Fry
34 Soviet Union
36 Caps
38 Gather
39 Colors
40 Bulb flower
41 Shut up
46 Measure of wood
47 Spanish "one"
48 Stole livestock
52 Promissory note
54 Organic compound
55 Kitchen appliance
56 Peeled
58 Listlessness
60 Not as wet
62 Roman emperor
64 Spoken
65 Grotto
66 De __ (anew)
67 Reverent
68 Path
70 Eastern Time

Puzzle #13

ACROSS

1 Branch of learning
5 Jewel studded
10 White lies
14 College head
15 Music used as practice
16 Fresh
17 Compel to go
18 Move forward
19 Notion
20 Like a dream
22 Wander
23 Km/h
24 Meet
26 Fire remains
27 Sore
30 Pawn
33 Either of the two side petals of a flower in the legume family
35 Afloat
37 Grocery bag (2 wds.)
42 Exploiter
43 Gorilla
44 Dice
45 Person
49 Fee
50 Director (abbr.)
51 Snip
53 Still
54 College football conference (abbr.)
57 Compass point
59 Grease
61 Goody
63 Nocturnal illumination
69 Green Gables dweller
70 Guts
71 Swain
72 Fish catchers
73 Lets out
74 Fiber
75 Horse's gait
76 French city
77 Domain

DOWN

1 Attention-Deficit Hyperactive Disorder (abbr.)
2 Bring up
3 Narration
4 Purloin
5 Bellhops
6 Decorative needle case
7 Washed-up
8 Brims
9 __-ball
10 Comely
11 Large Asian nation
12 __ up (makes bigger)
13 Path cut through grass
21 Car speed
22 Cafe
25 Ingest
27 Tropical island
28 Association (abbr.)
29 Accomplishment
31 Attired
32 Destroyed
34 Account (abbr.)
36 Dry
38 Scorch
39 Keep afloat
40 Apt
41 Money (German)
46 Contended
47 Internal Revenue Service
48 Queen of beasts
52 Cubic centimeter
54 __ -garde
55 Less coarse
56 Major division in a long poem
58 Nail filing board
60 African country
62 Bird's home
64 Brand of sandwich cookie
65 Kiln
66 Cogged wheel
67 Bunny
68 Sandwich fish
70 Football assoc.

Puzzle #14

ACROSS

1 Afresh
5 Beginning of Greek alphabet
10 Some (2 wds.)
14 Computer memory unit
15 Eyeshade
16 Maize
17 Sauteed veal cutlets
19 Sailors
20 Close to the ground
21 Elliptic
23 Rip-off
26 Female horses
28 Workplace
31 European sea eagle
32 Mr.s
33 Pride
34 Joseph's elder son
37 Goaded
39 W
40 Engage
42 Grown
45 White-faced red cattle
49 Tub
50 Hardships
53 Sailor's yes
54 East northeast
55 Improve
56 Spread
58 Frizzy
60 Mold
61 Royal treasury
63 Erosion formed cliff
69 Cut of beef
70 Chatty
71 Enclosed section of window
72 Christmas
73 Falls
74 Elm

DOWN

1 Abdominal muscles (abbr.)
2 Big Apple (abbr.)
3 Terminal abbr.
4 Ancient sinks
5 Declare openly
6 Brim
7 Pounds per square inch
8 Accolades
9 Movie "__ Runs Through It" (2 wds.)
10 Accounting Depatment (abbr.)
11 Front leg
12 Bard's before
13 West northwest
18 Dozens
22 Relieve of anxiety
23 Border
24 Time period
25 Lodge
26 Get together
27 Tree
29 Grow older
30 Chassis
32 Mountain Standard Time
35 Leather worker's tool
36 Subordinate ruler
38 Umpire
40 Pack
41 Tax agency
42 Street abbr.
43 Newsman Rather
44 Knife
45 Term of affection
46 Rowing tool
47 Grain
48 Water
51 About to occur
52 Spring
56 Drink slowly
57 Try to seduce
59 Inflammatory disease
60 Removes the water
61 Travel
62 Note of debt
64 Cash with order (abr.)
65 Viper
66 Hearing part
67 North northeast
68 __-ball

Puzzle #15

ACROSS

1 Parent groups
5 Land mass
9 Sketched
13 Papery
14 Schism
15 Midwestern state
16 Dress
17 Singing group
18 Always
19 Depress
21 Who you give gifts to
23 Type of tea
24 Capital of Western Samoa
25 Native American tribe member
28 Globes
31 Excited
32 Not quiet
34 Restaurant
36 Division (abbr.)
37 Wrath
38 Rio de Janeiro
39 Sledge
41 Sanctify
43 US liquid unit
44 Endows
46 Gold finder's phrase
48 Make secure
49 Dole out
50 Clusters
53 Hated
57 N.A. Indian
58 __ Lee (pie brand name)
60 Bod
61 Greek for "contest"
62 Speak
63 TV award
64 Ping __ (paddle game)
65 Cat cries
66 Salty water masses

DOWN

1 Posttraumatic stress disorder
2 Tai
3 Ventilates
4 Shooting covertly
5 Plant louse
6 Hole
7 Caesar's three
8 Wasting away of body
9 Bruce Willis movie
10 Stray
11 Water pitcher
12 Battles
14 Test
20 Frost
22 Knot
24 Recesses
25 Part of a football player's gear
26 Smart
27 Like cloth
28 Kings
29 Strange
30 Walk stealthily
33 Oil tanker
35 Small particle
40 Stopping up
41 Bloom
42 Buzz
43 Mashes
45 Jazz
47 Native American tribe
49 Animal products
50 Bloke
51 Company symbol
52 Onto
53 Plot
54 Very large book
55 Austin novel
56 24 hour periods
59 Be

Puzzle #16

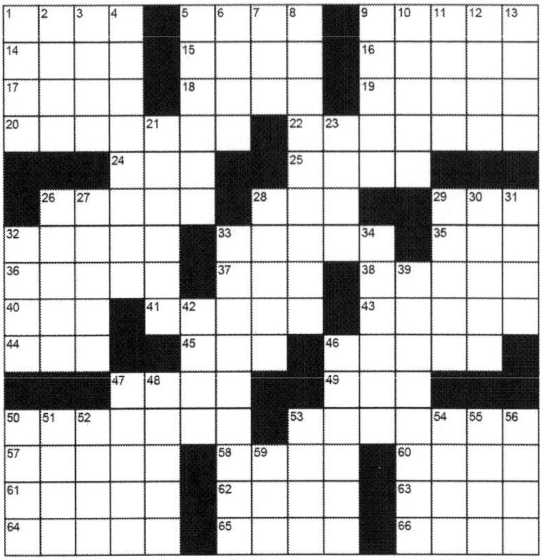

ACROSS

1 Animal feet
5 Second letter of the greek alphabet
9 Vaunt
14 Organization of Petroleum Exporting Countries
15 Absent without leave
16 Sound of a sneeze
17 Despot
18 Seethe
19 Sea animal's home
20 Two from each state
22 Worried
24 Pencil's pal
25 Egyptian river
26 Lower parts of faces
28 Cutting tool
29 Expert
32 Stadium
33 Book by Homer
35 Titan
36 Rule
37 Not (refix)
38 Goofed
40 Disks
41 Offering
43 Destitute
44 Fiery
45 Drink
46 Smears
47 A cozy room (2 wds.)
49 Canoe propeller
50 Avows
53 South American country
57 Yellow flower
58 Movie star
60 Window ledge
61 Country estate
62 Ballot
63 Women's magazine
64 What a hunted racoon is
65 Zeal
66 Back talk

DOWN

1 Pans
2 Church part
3 Deprive of mother's milk
4 Skinning
5 Band leaders instruments
6 Pitcher
7 Digit
8 Inexpensive purple garnet
9 Fundamental
10 Red pigment
11 Excuse me!
12 Lone
13 Said
21 Roomer
23 Ms. Minelli
26 Doctrine
27 Armed robbery
28 Hawaiian 'hello'
29 Go together
30 Dorm dwellers
31 Swirl
32 Flex
33 Concentrated
34 Abnegation
39 States again
42 Detail
46 Material
47 Hallway
48 Nymph
50 Advertisement (abbr.)
51 Balmy
52 Smooth nails
53 Wine bottle
54 Capital of Vanuatu
55 Evils
56 Brews
59 Pain unit

Puzzle #17

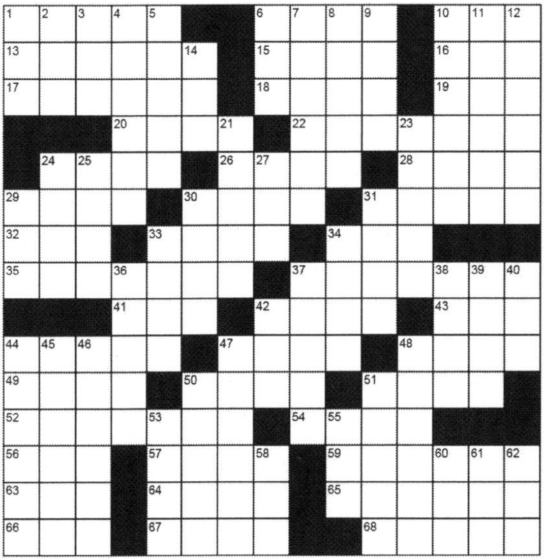

ACROSS

1 Piece of land
6 Capital of Norway
10 Certified public accountant
13 Verify
15 Beech
16 Movie 2001's talking computer
17 Now Iran
18 North Atlantic Treaty Organization
19 Entire
20 Artist Chagall
22 Outlying area
24 Chunk
26 Chopping tools
28 Russia
29 Prejudice
30 Native ruler in Africa
31 Greek island
32 __ A Small World...
33 Lotion brand
34 What a nurse gives
35 Irritatedly
37 African language
41 American Cancer Society (abbr.)
42 Radar target
43 Hustle
44 Dye by hand
47 Proximo abbr.
48 Hulk
49 Billions of years
50 Glean
51 Father's sister
52 Clenched your teeth
54 Omelette need
56 Bad (prefix)
57 Opaque gem
59 Excites
63 Snacked
64 DNA component
65 "__ a Mockingbird" (2 wds.)
66 Web
67 Singing voice
68 Absurd

DOWN

1 Cooking measurement
2 Fear
3 April (abbr.)
4 Universe
5 Trio
6 Hold
7 Latherer
8 Water lily
9 Aroma
10 __ longue
11 Whitest
12 Invite
14 Sticky black substance
21 Toyota car
23 Pitch forward
24 Quote
25 Young girl
27 Twelve
29 Fraction
30 Snaky fish
31 Thunder __
33 Punt
34 Stick candy bar brand
36 Defile
37 Hill
38 Flatten
39 Lucre
40 Computer makers
42 Women's undergarment
44 Stolen money distributor
45 Supply oxygen
46 Loo
47 Bookworm
48 Capital of Zambia
50 Drive away
51 Glowing
53 Roman garments
55 Garner
58 Constellation
60 Twitch
61 Deer relative
62 Tricky

Puzzle #18

ACROSS

1 Bunsen burner
5 Coke
9 Harvest
13 Bust
14 Do a dance
15 Polish
16 Object
17 Water retention
18 Coupe
19 Home to Denver and Boulder
21 Subatomic particle
23 Depend
24 Glen
25 Adopt
28 Foaming
31 Desert condition
32 Valley's partners
34 Reference point
36 Free of
37 Christmas month
38 Cow sound
39 Take the rind off
41 Satiny
43 Raps lightly
44 Wanderer
46 Waits
48 Even
49 Taste
50 N. American river
53 Turn in again
57 Exotic
58 Superior
60 Weightless
61 For__
62 Down duck
63 Clunk
64 Hand
65 Mob activity
66 Beano

DOWN

1 Great
2 Band formed in 1977
3 Christmas carol
4 Armed
5 Carrier
6 Margarine
7 Long-term memory
8 Flowers
9 Charlie_____
10 Defeat
11 Upon
12 Gofer
14 Luxury
20 Representative
22 Shade tree
24 "__ et decorum est..."
25 American Association of Retired Persons (abbr.)
26 Wailed
27 Beverage
28 Sneer
29 Rover
30 Search in the dark
33 Left out of gear
35 Green seedless plant
40 Throws trash
41 Steel worker
42 German ruler
43 Drape holder
45 Tally
47 Energy unit
49 Mother
50 Secondary
51 Volcanic rock
52 Greek god of war
53 Remake
54 1.6 kilometers
55 Press
56 Typing error
59 Roman three

Puzzle #19

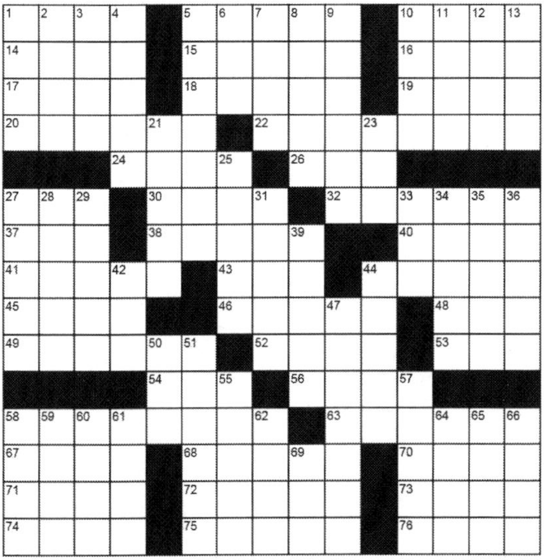

ACROSS

1 Wash
5 Influential person
10 False bible god
14 Opera solo
15 Non-confining
16 Desire
17 Spool
18 Seraph
19 Move while sleeping
20 Capital of the Bahamas
22 Halting progress
24 Handout
26 Whichever
27 Short-term memory
30 Stretched
32 Colorful Mexican shawl
37 Bind
38 Quaking tree
40 Computer picture button
41 More able
43 Environmental protection agency (abbr)
44 Graceful
45 Baseball glove
46 Exercise authority over
48 10 meters (abbr. for dekameter)
49 Programming language
52 Tied
53 Allege
54 Telegraphic signal
56 Canal
58 Long, dramatic musical composition
63 Reminiscence
67 Undiluted
68 Asian country
70 Entreaty
71 Eve's garden
72 Add
73 Bluish green
74 Learning thermostat
75 Turkey dwellers
76 Past times

DOWN

1 Farm building
2 Location
3 Knots
4 Shampoo brand
5 Injuries
6 Charged particle
7
8 Very tiny animal
9 Hose
10 Prime
11 Opposed
12 Tel __ (Israel's capital)
13 Harp
21 Lord's table
23 Seed bread
25 First-rate
27 Stomp
28 Leg bone
29 What cheese does
31 Wigwam
33 Set up
34 Hydrochloric and nitric, for example
35 Folk dance
36 Foe
39 Unsuspecting
42 And so forth
44 Red headed orphan
47 Berlin Dwellers
50 Hoopla
51 A cowboy's rope
55 Eastern religion
57 Take everything out
58 Agape
59 Impolite
60 Greek god of war
61 Cabana
62 Smell
64 Fake butter
65 Raise
66 Harvard's rival
69 Annoy

Puzzle #20

ACROSS

1 Furthest back
4 Annoyances
9 Swab
12 Become less distinct
14 Purple vegetable
15 Torah table
16 Skeletal part
17 Tell
18 Sign
19 Confirm again
21 Inching forward
23 Estimated time of arrival
24 Grain
25 Remain
28 Sheet
31 Looked at
34 Zany
36 Point
38 Newspaper
40 Yes
41 Flips over
43 Motor vehicle
44 Wooden leg
45 Inquire
46 Lever moved by another part
48 Place to sit down
51 Poisonous snake
53 Meshes
54 MI
56 Beret
58 Large shrimp
61 Becoming electrically charged
66 Bass horn
67 Flaxen
69 Dark
70 Begin
71 Oarsman
72 One of Columbus' ships
73 Pacific Time
74 Informed
75 Condensation

DOWN

1 Reduce (abbr.)
2 Ice sheet
3 Bonito
4 Suggest
5 Capture
6 Thailand
7 Child
8 Make a face
9 Less than usual in size, power or character
10 Prayer ending
11 Slamming sound
13 Game official
15 Bogy
20 Soft white cheese
22 Change color
25 Gets out of sleep
26 Expression
27 Frosty
29 Small birds
30 Yang's partner
32 Burst outward
33 Comes from the Date Palm
34 Swab
35 School group
37 Mountain Time
39 Gained
42 America
43 Baboon
47 Negative (prefix)
49 Capital of Jordan
50 Gratuity mark
52 Talker
55 Sign of the scales
57 Giant in 'Princess Bride'
58 Quit
59 Mugs
60 To incite
61 Hawkeye State
62 Type of Buddhism
63 As previously cited
64 Not any
65 Chew
68 Not high

Puzzle #21

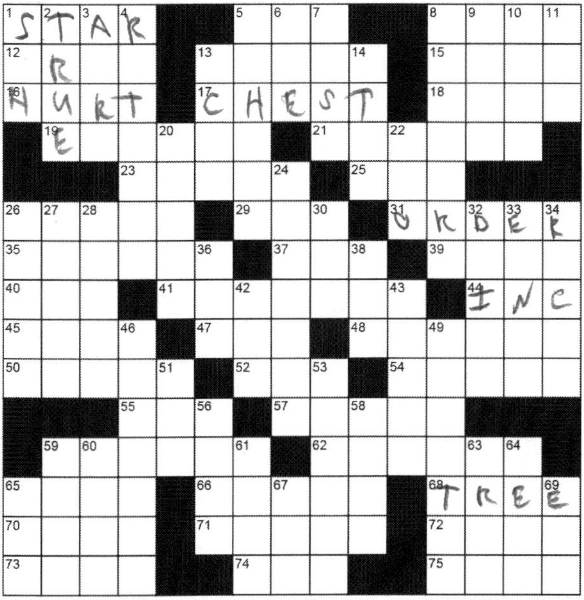

ACROSS

1 Celebrity
5 Sibling
8 Clinton's Vice President
12 Little pigment
13 Map collection
15 Avouch
16 __ matter
17 Treasure
18 Maimed
19 Artist of illusion
21 Shame
23 Fire holder
25 Wrong (prefix)
26 State capital
29 That woman
31 Religious divisions
35 Weathered
37 Official
39 Tub spread
40 Creative work
41 Plight
44 Business title ending
45 Latin "in all"
47 Animal doctor
48 City
50 Weapon
52 Facial twitch
54 Nobleman
55 Cation
57 __ for (took care of)
59 Tiger (2 wds.)
62 Wirelesses
65 Lotion brand
66 Wilt
68 Leaf maker
70 Make headway
71 Analyze
72 Moray
73 Kiss
74 Moray
75 Dummy

DOWN

1 Resort hotel
2 Fib
3 __ for the poor
4 Responded
5 Gravy thickener
6 Ailing
7 Data transmission rate
8 Italian astronomer
9 Egg-shaped
10 Italian capital
11 Ram's mate
13 Maintain
14 Appear
20 __ in (focused)
22 Foreign Agricultural Service
24 Dissenter from church
26 Couches
27 Native American Weapon
28 Gambling game
30 Rock group
32 Chink
33 Tight
34 Argyle
36 Division (abbr.)
38 Madagascar franc (abbr.)
42 Permit
43 Additional
46 Sources
49 Examined
51 Physician
53 Penzoil is this (2 wds.)
56 Zip
58 Attentive
59 Boyfriend
60 Part of the eye
61 Opp. of false
63 Brand of sandwich cookie
64 Market
65 Former USSR's secret police
67 Lyric poem
69 Eastern Time

Puzzle #22

ACROSS

1 Fence
5 Kismet
9 Poke
13 Mexican sandwich
14 Speak without preparation
15 American river
16 Scene division
17 Toast leftover
18 Adult female
19 Government
21 Cell division process
23 Earns
25 Irritation
26 Government agency
29 Fades
31 Skate
34 However
35 Cake topping
37 Sheltered inlet
39 Rodeo bull
41 __ Pits
42 Fable writer
43 Very large truck
44 Sagas
46 Obtain or create, but just barely
47 Painter Richard
50 Espy
51 Perceive
52 A person regarded as despicable
54 Mud
56 Loving
59 Crops
63 Priggish
64 Gigantic
66 Naughty or __ (what Santa checks)
67 Stay
68 Judged
69 Soon
70 Paradise
71 9th month
72 Mouth off

DOWN

1 Nova
2 Walk back and forth
3 Acting (abbr.)
4 Violinist's need
5 Not JFK
6 Astringent
7 Life and __
8 Declining
9 Winter's longest night
10 Citizen
11 Acquired Immune Deficiency Syndrome (abbr.)
12 Male
14 Vinegar's acid
20 Doctor
22 Lubricate
24 Strike hard
26 Tides
27 Mush up
28 Tiny particles
30 Joins together
32 Medication amounts
33 Arouse
36 Grasps
38 Dueling sword
40 Part of atmosphere
42 Bustling
45 Caged
48 Serving of corn
49 Leg extensions
53 Snag
55 Type of eclipse
56 Among
57 Ranch guy
58 Clutch
60 One of Columbus' ships
61 Economics abrv.
62 Mailed
63 South by east
65 Comprehend

Puzzle #23

ACROSS

1 Painter of melting clocks
5 Muslim's God
10 Secondhand
14 Eagerness
15 Apollo
16 Hurting
17 Fruit that has been pressed for winemaking
18 Drove
19 Actor Woody
20 Mistake
22 Quaff
24 Time zone
25 Asian starling
27 Sacred song
29 Feet wear
32 Wash off
35 Biblical "you"
38 Bullfight cheer
39 Looking
40 Honey abr.
41 Insult
43 Zag's partner
44 Seniors
46 Those who make the food laws (abbr.)
47 Antes
48 Shouts
49 Needle worker
51 Marry secretly
54 Stamp
57 United Parcel Service
59 Lowest point
62 Hip
64 Loch __ monster
66 Tempts
68 Wall support
69 Portion
70 Quick bread
71 Gas burner
72 Black stone
73 Gossiper
74 Look

DOWN

1 Interbreeding population within a species
2 Dismay
3 One of the Stooges
4 Burnt fragrance
5 Advertisements
6 Ribald
7 Prevaricator
8 A vacation (2 wds.)
9 Religious songs
10 North American country
11 Make somber
12 Times
13 Indent
21 Morse code "T"
23 Weight measurement
26 Horses feet
28 Movie star Taylor
30 Pixie
31 Slaves
33 Vexation
34 Omelette ingredient
35 Those people
36 Eyelet
37 Infinitely
39 Chew like a rodent
41 Malicious burning
42 Poem of praise
45 Annex
47 Grazes
50 Terminal abbr.
52 Debilitating influence
53 Elicit
55 Dull
56 Crop
57 Unclip
58 Lowest in rank
60 Smooth
61 Lease
63 Cheese
65 Gender
67 Body of water

Puzzle #24

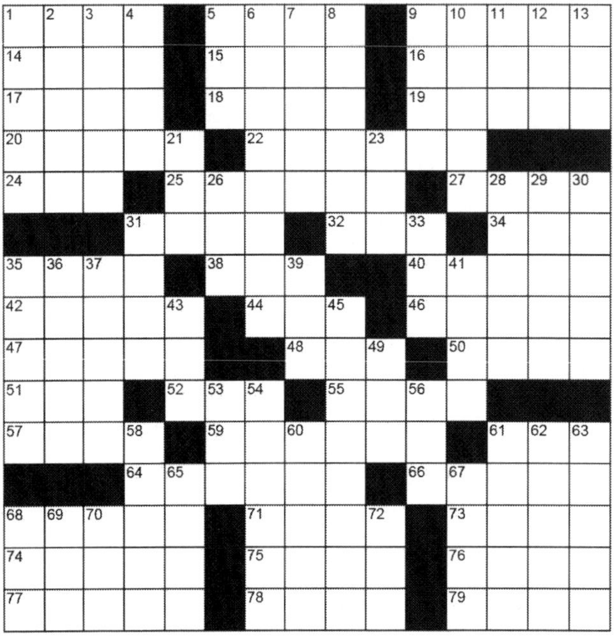

ACROSS

1 Reduce (abbr.)
5 Apt
9 Book by Homer
14 Frock
15 Smooth
16 Slang term for man
17 Small ground plot
18 Dictator (abbr.)
19 Rim of spoked wheel
20 Car manufacturer
22 Martin Luther King Jr., for example
24 May
25 Lost
27 Indecent language
31 Portend
32 Terminal abbr.
34 Government agency
35 Ditto
38 Mountain Time
40 Caste
42 Tray of cookies
44 Body of water
46 Belief
47 Stop
48 Loose gown worn at mass
50 Lawyer (abbr.)
51 Chick holder
52 Desert
55 Seaweed
57 Meditation
59 First courses
61 Cooking measurement
64 Not unleaded or regular
66 National capital
68 Chide
71 Tack
73 Off-Broadway award
74 Month
75 Wood tool
76 Coke
77 Lumpy
78 Secondhand
79 Cologne (Gr.)

DOWN

1 Molded salad
2 Light weight wood
3 Strength
4 Round cracker brand
5 Help
6 Without a brim
7 Specific
8 Main dish
9 Unpredictable
10 Jeers
11 Ailing
12 Entire
13 Part of a week
21 Alien's spaceship
23 Explosive
26 Admiral (abbr.)
28 Intended
29 Miffed
30 Delicious
31 Dark beer
33 Skit
35 Church
36 Slow (musical term)
37 Canned chili brand
39 British drink
41 Bounce
43 That woman
45 Chemical process
49 Bedroom furniture
53 Wield
54 Capital of the Bahamas
56 Hallucinogen
58 Speak without preparation
60 Guides
61 No-no
62 Forte
63 Praise
65 Lazily
67 Pawn
68 __ Francisco
69 Computer part
70 Bolus
72 Headed

Puzzle #25

ACROSS

1 Noodle
6 Snacked
9 Bowed stringed instrument
13 Ancient Indian
14 Drag
15 Store passageway
16 Insertion mark
17 Chick holder
18 Valleys
19 Eagerness
20 Worried
22 Aurora
23 Representative
24 Soaked
25 Pull
27 Resource
29 Marry
33 North American country
34 Bullfight cheer
35 Trigonometry
36 Reproduce
39 Annex
40 Horse
41 Church song
42 Last
43 Cry softly
44 Relies, with "on"
46 __ forward
49 Do business
50 Morse code dot
51 That man
53 Type of meat
56 Large South American river
58 Pater
59 Held high
61 Animal doctor
62 Poor quality fish
63 Biblical prophet
64 Bard's before
65 Figure
66 Fast airplanes
67 Sward
68 Alders

DOWN

1 Horse that paces
2 Rhododendron
3 Belts
4 Adolescent
5 Skit
6 Aleutian
7 Pulls
8 Yolk protector
9 By way of
10 Island
11 Tub spread
12 Fewer
15 Tally (2 wds.)
20 Soft white cheese
21 Console
24 Compass point
26 Dry skin need
28 Laid in the sun
30 Pot
31 Be seated
32 Pride
34 Hoary
36 Doctoral degree
37 Grain
38 Brat
39 Brings into bondage
40 Sulk
42 Cheese
43 Jaw point
45 Under, poetically
47 Make a payment
48 Nonconformist
50 Pampered
52 Ship's sail holders
53 Pilgrimage to Mecca
54 Healing plant
55 Montana (abbr.)
57 Zip
58 Set of 2
60 Foreign Agricultural Service
62 Central daylight time

Puzzle #1

Solution:

O	F	F		M	I	A	M	I		S	P	A	D	E
P	E	A		A	R	I	E	S		H	A	L	E	D
E	E	L		T	I	D	A	L		O	R	A	N	G
C	L	A	M		S	E	L	E	C	T		S	T	Y
			U	G	H				E	G	G			
	M	O	D	E	M	S		C	O	U	N	T	S	
B	I	N		L	E	M	U	R		N	A	A	C	P
U	N	I	T		N	A	M	E	S		W	I	R	E
S	C	O	U	R		S	P	A	C	E		L	A	P
	E	N	M	E	S	H		M	O	N	I	S	M	
			S	R	I				L	E	O			
E	R	E		E	R	A	S	E	D		U	C	L	A
C	O	T	T	A		R	A	D	I	I		I	I	I
H	O	U	N	D		A	G	E	N	T		T	E	N
O	M	I	T	S		B	A	N	G	S		E	S	T

Puzzle #2

Solution:

S	O	L	D		G	Y	P	S		S	E	D	A	N
A	R	E	A		R	O	L	L		A	D	I	E	U
M	A	N	Y		A	G	U	A		D	I	V	O	T
B	L	T		E	N	I	G	M	A		F	A	N	S
A	B	O	A	R	D				I	V	Y			
			C	I	A		D	E	M	I		O	D	E
	E	P	H	E	M	E	R	A		E	N	D	O	W
A	G	U	E			C	U	R			O	O	Z	E
R	O	N	D	O		O	M	N	I	V	O	R	E	
M	S	T		W	I	N	S		G	A	S			
			E	L	L				N	I	E	C	E	S
A	P	E	X		L	E	N	T	I	L		U	N	O
C	R	A	T	E		R	I	O	T		A	S	S	N
T	E	R	R	A		A	N	T	E		T	H	U	G
S	P	L	A	T		S	E	E	D		E	Y	E	S

Puzzle #3

Solution:

F	I	C	H	U		G	O	U	P		A	P	S	E
I	S	L	A	M		U	R	S	A		C	R	A	M
S	L	U	M	P		E	A	S	Y		T	U	T	U
T	E	E	M		A	S	L		R	H	O	D	E	S
			O	D	D	S		M	O	O	R	E	D	
S	P	A	C	E	S		D	I	L	L				
H	A	W	K	S		S	A	D	L	Y		B	I	C
A	R	O	S	E		C	N	S		C	I	R	C	A
G	E	L		R	H	E	T	T		I	C	I	E	R
				T	U	N	E		S	T	E	E	D	S
	I	N	F	E	S	T		D	R	Y	S			
B	R	O	A	D	S		T	A	I		H	A	L	O
A	K	I	N		I	C	O	N		P	E	C	A	N
L	E	S	T		E	P	I	C		R	E	L	I	C
I	D	E	A		S	A	L	E		E	T	U	D	E

Puzzle #4

Solution:

I	O	T	A			A	L	P	O		P	A	T	E
O	V	A	L		S	H	E	A	F		E	G	I	S
W	E	N	T		M	A	N	E	T		R	U	D	E
A	N	G	O	R	A		D	A	H	O	M	E	Y	
			S	E	C	T		N	I	C	E			
S	E	A		S	K	E	W		S	T	A	B	S	
P	I	G		I	S	A	A	C			T	R	E	E
A	D	O	R	N		M	I	L		B	E	A	R	D
M	E	R	E			S	T	A	R	E		K	E	G
	R	A	D	A	R		S	N	A	G		E	R	E
			F	L	A	K		K	I	E	V			
	C	A	R	A	C	A	S		S	T	E	R	N	A
T	O	F	U		K	H	A	K	I		N	E	A	T
S	A	R	I		E	L	F	I	N		U	N	T	O
P	L	O	T		T	O	E	D			S	T	O	P

Puzzle #5

Solution:

A	B	E	L			P	E	W			D	R	A	B
P	A	V	E		L	Y	R	I	C		A	E	R	O
T	R	I	X		I	T	A	L	Y		V	A	M	P
	E	L	I	J	A	H		E	A	S	I	L	Y	
			C	A	R	O	M		N	O	N			
A	S	S	O	C		N	I	P		S	C	A	B	S
B	U	E	N	O	S		N	A	B		I	D	E	A
A	R	T		B	I	T	U	M	E	N		L	A	G
F	L	U	X		S	U	E		D	I	V	I	N	E
T	Y	P	E	D		G	N	P		H	O	B	O	S
			R	I	O		D	E	V	I	L			
	K	I	O	S	K	S		O	I	L	C	A	N	
J	I	N	X		R	A	S	P	S		A	R	E	A
O	N	C	E		A	L	U	L	A		N	A	R	Y
B	E	A	D			E	N	E			O	B	O	E

Puzzle #6

Solution:

P	A	T	E	■	R	A	S	P	■	B	A	S	S	O
A	G	A	R	■	O	B	I	E	■	E	L	B	O	W
T	A	X	I	■	B	I	R	R	■	D	O	W	S	E
S	P	E	C	K	■	D	E	M	I	S	E	■	■	■
Y	E	S	■	P	H	A	S	I	C	■	S	O	A	P
■	■	■	S	H	I	N	■	T	E	E	■	C	P	A
R	O	T	C	■	M	C	G	■	■	O	S	C	A	R
O	R	I	O	N	■	E	A	T	■	S	H	U	C	K
A	B	A	T	E	■	■	B	R	A	■	O	R	E	S
D	I	R	■	T	E	N	■	I	N	S	T	■	■	■
S	T	A	B	■	S	A	N	C	T	A	■	F	C	A
■	■	■	O	S	P	R	E	Y	■	C	H	A	L	K
P	A	Y	U	P	■	R	I	C	K	■	O	D	O	R
S	H	A	L	E	■	O	G	L	E	■	M	E	M	O
T	A	M	E	D	■	W	H	E	Y	■	E	S	P	N

Puzzle #7

Solution:

S	T	A	B		B	O	R	G		E	A	T	U	P
C	U	T	E		A	D	A	R		S	L	O	P	E
A	L	O	E		N	O	P	E		P	I	T	O	N
N	I	L		M	A	R	T	Y	R		B	O	N	N
S	P	L	E	E	N				I	I	I			
			B	O	A		S	H	O	W		S	P	A
	D	R	O	W	S	I	L	Y		O	G	L	E	D
M	I	E	N			D	I	M			N	U	T	S
P	R	A	Y	S		O	M	N	I	V	O	R	E	
H	E	M		O	N	L	Y		M	A	M			
			P	S	I				P	I	E	N	U	T
M	I	T	E		P	Y	T	H	O	N		O	L	E
E	R	A	S	E		W	O	O	S		R	I	C	A
S	A	X	O	N		C	O	P	E		U	S	E	S
A	N	I	S	E		A	L	E	S		M	E	R	E

Puzzle #8

Solution:

S	P	O	R	E		Y	A	M			V	A	N	E
P	I	P	E	S		A	G	E		H	O	L	E	D
E	S	T	E	E		C	U	E		A	W	A	R	D
A	C	I	D		K	H	A	K	I	S		S	O	Y
R	E	M		S	A	T		N	O	T	E			
	S	A	I	T	H			E	T	E	R	N	A	L
			D	I	N		U	S	A		R	U	N	E
W	A	F	E	R		C	P	S		P	I	N	T	O
P	L	E	A		P	A	S		H	E	N			
M	I	D	T	E	R	M			A	R	G	O	T	
			E	R	I	E		E	M	U		W	A	S
I	C	Y		O	G	R	E	S	S		A	L	M	A
F	L	O	O	D		O	U	T		A	X	I	A	L
F	U	G	U	E		O	R	E		L	I	S	L	E
Y	E	A	R			N	O	R		A	S	H	E	S

Puzzle #9

Solution:

H	A	I	K	U		C	A	P	T		U	M	B	O
A	U	D	I	T		H	E	R	O		S	U	R	F
S	T	O	L	E		I	R	O	N		S	L	A	T
P	O	L	L		B	L	O	W	I	T		E	V	E
			E	T	U	I			G	O	D	S	O	N
S	T	E	R	N	O			A	H	O	Y			
E	E	L		T	Y	P	I	S	T		E	V	E	N
G	A	S	H			A	C	S			S	A	V	E
O	L	E	O		T	R	E	N	D	Y		S	I	B
			W	O	R	K			R	A	T	T	L	E
M	A	S	E	R	U			T	Y	P	E			
U	F	O		B	I	R	T	H	S		E	B	O	N
M	I	N	E		S	E	A	R		S	N	O	R	E
P	R	I	X		M	E	R	E		A	S	H	E	S
S	E	C	T		S	L	E	W		G	Y	R	O	S

Puzzle #10

Solution:

S	T	E	W		A	C	M	E		B	R	A	V	O
L	I	M	A		L	O	A	D		L	U	G	E	R
O	B	E	Y		D	O	L	E		T	B	O	N	E
T	I	N		F	E	L	I	N	E		E	N	D	S
H	A	D	F	U	N				E	R	N			
			A	R	T		S	A	G	A		S	P	A
	C	H	E	Y	E	N	N	E		N	E	P	A	L
A	L	A	N			O	U	R			M	I	N	T
L	I	R	A	S		S	C	O	R	N	I	N	G	
B	P	M		R	E	E	K		E	E	L			
			M	I	N				L	A	Y	I	N	G
A	B	L	E		E	N	D	E	A	R		T	I	E
B	E	I	N	G		A	A	R	P		P	A	G	E
C	E	A	S	E		P	T	A	S		A	L	E	S
S	P	R	A	T		E	A	S	E		L	Y	R	E

Puzzle #11

Solution:

F	L	A	B		S	M	A	L	L		N	A	B	S
L	E	V	Y		P	O	L	I	O		E	D	I	T
E	V	I	L		A	L	O	N	G		B	I	T	E
D	I	S	A	G	R	E	E	D		S	N	E	E	R
			W	A	R			A	F	C		U	R	N
C	A	B		P	O	T	S		D	A	H			
H	U	L	A		W	A	T	E	R	M	E	L	O	N
A	T	O	P			P	A	R			M	A	K	E
R	O	B	I	T	U	S	S	I	N		P	U	R	E
			A	R	M		H	E	I	R		D	A	D
D	E	N		U	P	S			G	E	M			
A	D	O	R	E		W	I	S	H	F	U	L	L	Y
Z	U	N	I		G	E	N	E	T		S	I	A	M
E	C	O	N		N	A	S	A	L		E	R	I	C
D	E	S	K		U	R	T	S	Y		D	A	D	A

Puzzle #12

Solution:

F	L	A	B		A	H	E	A	D		P	A	I	L
R	I	V	E		L	E	M	U	R		O	N	C	E
O	M	I	T		L	A	I	T	Y		K	N	I	T
M	O	V	E	D	U	P	T	O		H	Y	I	N	G
			L	A	D			S	P	Y		E	G	O
D	N	A		H	E	R	S		E	M	U			
R	O	L	L		S	E	A	M	A	N	S	H	I	P
A	N	T	I			S	U	E			S	U	R	E
W	O	O	D	C	U	T	T	E	R		R	E	I	N
			S	O	N		E	T	U	I		S	S	T
E	S	P		R	O	E			S	O	D			
S	T	A	N	D		N	O	C	T	U	R	N	A	L
T	O	R	E		E	N	R	O	L		I	O	W	A
E	V	E	R		S	U	A	V	E		E	V	E	N
R	E	D	O		T	I	L	E	D		R	O	D	E

Puzzle #13

Solution:

A	R	T	S	■	B	E	S	E	T	■	F	I	B	S
D	E	A	N	■	E	T	U	D	E	■	A	N	E	W
H	A	L	E	■	L	U	N	G	E	■	I	D	E	A
D	R	E	A	M	L	I	K	E	■	D	R	I	F	T
■	■	■	K	P	H	■	■	S	E	E	■	A	S	H
M	A	D	■	H	O	C	K	■	A	L	A	■	■	■
A	S	E	A	■	P	L	A	S	T	I	C	B	A	G
U	S	E	R	■	■	A	P	E	■	■	C	U	B	E
I	N	D	I	V	I	D	U	A	L	■	T	O	L	L
■	■	■	D	I	R	■	T	R	I	M	■	Y	E	T
A	F	C	■	E	S	E	■	■	O	I	L	■	■	■
V	I	A	N	D	■	M	O	O	N	L	I	G	H	T
A	N	N	E	■	N	E	R	V	E	■	B	E	A	U
N	E	T	S	■	F	R	E	E	S	■	Y	A	R	N
T	R	O	T	■	L	Y	O	N	S	■	A	R	E	A

Puzzle #14

Solution:

A	N	E	W		A	L	P	H	A		A	F	E	W
B	Y	T	E		V	I	S	O	R		C	O	R	N
S	C	A	L	L	O	P	I	N	I		C	R	E	W
			L	O	W			O	V	A	T	E		
H	E	I	S	T		M	A	R	E	S		L	A	B
E	R	N			M	E	S	S	R	S		E	G	O
M	A	N	A	S	S	E	H			U	R	G	E	D
			W	A	T	T		H	I	R	E			
A	D	U	L	T			H	E	R	E	F	O	R	D
V	A	T		R	I	G	O	R	S			A	Y	E
E	N	E		A	M	E	N	D		S	T	R	E	W
		N	A	P	P	Y			D	I	E			
F	I	S	C		E	S	C	A	R	P	M	E	N	T
L	O	I	N		N	E	W	S	Y		P	A	N	E
Y	U	L	E		D	R	O	P	S		T	R	E	E

Puzzle #15

Solution:

P	T	A	S			A	S	I	A		D	R	E	W
T	H	I	N		S	P	L	I	T		I	O	W	A
S	A	R	I		C	H	O	I	R		E	V	E	R
D	I	S	P	I	R	I	T		O	T	H	E	R	S
			I	C	E	D		A	P	I	A			
P	A	W	N	E	E		S	P	H	E	R	E	S	
A	G	O	G		N	O	I	S	Y		D	E	L	I
D	I	V				I	R	E				R	I	O
S	L	E	D		B	L	E	S	S		P	I	N	T
	E	N	A	B	L	E	S		E	U	R	E	K	A
			M	O	O	R		M	E	T	E			
C	L	U	M	P	S		D	E	T	E	S	T	E	D
H	O	P	I		S	A	R	A	H		S	O	M	A
A	G	O	N		O	R	A	T	E		E	M	M	Y
P	O	N	G		M	E	W	S			S	E	A	S

Puzzle #16

Solution:

P	A	W	S	■	B	E	T	A	■	B	O	A	S	T
O	P	E	C	■	A	W	O	L	■	A	C	H	O	O
T	S	A	R	■	T	E	E	M	■	S	H	E	L	L
S	E	N	A	T	O	R	■	A	L	A	R	M	E	D
■	■	■	P	E	N	■	■	N	I	L	E	■	■	■
■	C	H	I	N	S	■	A	D	Z	■	■	A	C	E
A	R	E	N	A	■	I	L	I	A	D	■	G	O	D
R	E	I	G	N	■	N	O	N	■	E	R	R	E	D
C	D	S	■	T	I	T	H	E	■	N	E	E	D	Y
H	O	T	■	■	T	E	A	■	W	I	P	E	S	■
■	■	■	A	D	E	N	■	■	O	A	R	■	■	■
A	F	F	I	R	M	S	■	B	O	L	I	V	I	A
D	A	I	S	Y	■	I	D	O	L	■	S	I	L	L
V	I	L	L	A	■	V	O	T	E	■	E	L	L	E
T	R	E	E	D	■	E	L	A	N	■	S	A	S	S

Puzzle #17

Solution:

T	R	A	C	T			O	S	L	O		C	P	A
S	U	P	O	R	T		W	O	O	D		H	A	L
P	E	R	S	I	A		N	A	T	O		A	L	L
			M	A	R	C		P	U	R	L	I	E	U
	C	L	O	D		A	X	E	S		U	S	S	R
B	I	A	S		E	M	I	R		C	R	E	T	E
I	T	S		K	E	R	I		T	L	C			
T	E	S	T	I	L	Y		S	W	A	H	I	L	I
			A	C	S		B	L	I	P		R	O	B
B	A	T	I	K		P	R	O	X		L	O	O	M
A	E	O	N		R	E	A	P		A	U	N	T	
G	R	I	T	T	E	D		E	G	G	S			
M	A	L		O	P	A	L		E	L	A	T	E	S
A	T	E		G	E	N	E		T	O	K	I	L	L
N	E	T		A	L	T	O			W	A	C	K	Y

Puzzle #18

Solution:

E	T	N	A			C	O	L	A		C	R	O	P
P	O	O	R		W	A	L	T	Z		H	O	N	E
I	T	E	M		E	D	E	M	A		A	U	T	O
C	O	L	O	R	A	D	O		L	E	P	T	O	N
			R	E	L	Y		D	E	L	L			
A	C	C	E	P	T		F	O	A	M	I	N	G	
A	R	I	D		H	I	L	L	S		N	O	R	M
R	I	D				D	E	C				M	O	O
P	E	E	L		S	L	E	E	K		T	A	P	S
	D	R	I	F	T	E	R		A	B	I	D	E	S
			T	I	E	D		B	I	T	E			
P	L	A	T	T	E		R	E	S	U	B	M	I	T
R	A	R	E		L	I	E	G	E		A	I	R	Y
E	V	E	R		E	I	D	E	R		C	L	O	P
P	A	S	S		R	I	O	T			K	E	N	O

Puzzle #19

Solution:

B	A	T	H		T	I	T	A	N		B	A	A	L
A	R	I	A		R	O	O	M	Y		E	N	V	Y
R	E	E	L		A	N	G	E	L		S	T	I	R
N	A	S	S	A	U		A	B	O	R	T	I	V	E
			A	L	M	S		A	N	Y				
S	T	M		T	A	U	T		S	E	R	A	P	E
T	I	E		A	S	P	E	N			I	C	O	N
A	B	L	E	R		E	P	A		A	G	I	L	E
M	I	T	T			R	E	I	G	N		D	K	M
P	A	S	C	A	L		E	V	E	N		S	A	Y
				D	A	H		E	R	I	E			
O	R	A	T	O	R	I	O		M	E	M	O	R	Y
P	U	R	E		I	N	D	I	A		P	L	E	A
E	D	E	N		A	D	O	R	N		T	E	A	L
N	E	S	T		T	U	R	K	S		Y	O	R	E

Puzzle #20

Solution:

A	F	T			P	E	S	T	S			D	A	B
B	L	U	R		O	N	I	O	N		B	E	M	A
B	O	N	E		S	T	A	T	E		O	M	E	N
R	E	A	F	F	I	R	M		E	D	G	I	N	G
				E	T	A			R	Y	E			
	W	A	I	T		P	L	Y		E	Y	E	D	
M	A	D	C	A	P		A	I	M			R	A	G
O	K	A	Y		T	U	R	N	S		A	U	T	O
P	E	G			A	S	K		T	A	P	P	E	T
	S	E	A	T		A	S	P		N	E	T	S	
			M	I	L			H	A	T				
S	C	A	M	P	I		I	O	N	I	Z	I	N	G
T	U	B	A		B	L	O	N	D		E	B	O	N
O	P	E	N		R	O	W	E	R		N	I	N	A
P	S	T			A	W	A	R	E			D	E	W

Puzzle #21

Solution:

S	T	A	R			S	I	B			G	O	R	E
P	A	L	E		A	T	L	A	S		A	V	O	W
A	L	M	A		V	A	L	U	E		L	A	M	E
	E	S	C	H	E	R		D	E	F	I	L	E	
			T	O	R	C	H		M	A	L			
S	A	L	E	M		H	E	R		S	E	C	T	S
E	R	O	D	E	D		R	E	F		O	L	E	O
A	R	T		D	I	L	E	M	M	A		I	N	C
T	O	T	O		V	E	T		G	D	A	N	S	K
S	W	O	R	D		T	I	C		D	U	K	E	S
			I	O	N		C	A	R	E	D			
	B	I	G	C	A	T		R	A	D	I	O	S	
K	E	R	I		D	R	O	O	P		T	R	E	E
G	A	I	N		A	U	D	I	T		E	E	L	S
B	U	S	S			E	E	L			D	O	L	T

Puzzle #22

Solution:

S	P	A	R			F	A	T	E		S	T	A	B
T	A	C	O		A	D	L	I	B		O	H	I	O
A	C	T	S		C	R	U	M	B		L	A	D	Y
R	E	G	I	M	E		M	E	I	O	S	I	S	
			N	E	T	S		S	N	I	T			
E	P	A		D	I	M	S		G	L	I	D	E	
B	U	T		I	C	I	N	G			C	O	V	E
B	R	O	N	C		T	A	R		A	E	S	O	P
S	E	M	I			E	P	I	C	S		E	K	E
	E	S	T	E	S		S	P	O	T		S	E	E
			R	A	T	S		S	O	I	L			
	A	D	O	R	I	N	G		P	R	U	N	E	S
S	M	U	G		L	A	R	G	E		N	I	C	E
B	I	D	E		T	R	I	E	D		A	N	O	N
E	D	E	N		S	E	P	T			R	A	N	T

Puzzle #23

Solution:

D	A	L	I		A	L	L	A	H		U	S	E	D
E	L	A	N		D	E	I	T	Y		S	O	R	E
M	A	R	C		S	W	A	R	M		A	L	A	N
E	R	R	E	D		D	R	I	N	K		E	S	T
	M	Y	N	A	H			P	S	A	L	M		
			S	H	O	E	S			R	I	N	S	E
T	H	E	E		O	L	E		G	A	Z	I	N	G
H	O	N		A	F	F	R	O	N	T		Z	I	G
E	L	D	E	R	S		F	D	A		B	E	T	S
Y	E	L	L	S			S	E	W	E	R			
		E	L	O	P	E			S	T	O	M	P	
U	P	S		N	A	D	I	R		A	W	A	R	E
N	E	S	S		L	U	R	E	S		S	T	U	D
D	O	L	E		S	C	O	N	E		E	T	N	A
O	N	Y	X		Y	E	N	T	A		S	E	E	M

Puzzle #24

Solution:

A	B	B	R		A	B	L	E		I	L	I	A	D
S	A	R	I		I	R	O	N		F	E	L	L	A
P	L	A	T		D	I	C	T		F	E	L	L	Y
I	S	U	Z	U		M	A	R	T	Y	R			
C	A	N		F	A	L	L	E	N		S	M	U	T
			B	O	D	E		E	T	A		E	P	A
A	L	S	O		M	S	T			C	L	A	S	S
B	A	T	C	H		S	E	A		T	E	N	E	T
B	R	A	K	E			A	L	B		A	T	T	Y
E	G	G		R	U	N		K	E	L	P			
Y	O	G	A		S	A	L	A	D	S		T	S	P
			D	I	E	S	E	L		D	H	A	K	A
S	C	O	L	D		S	A	I	L		O	B	I	E
A	P	R	I	L		A	D	Z	E		C	O	L	A
N	U	B	B	Y		U	S	E	D		K	O	L	N

Puzzle #25

Solution:

P	A	S	T	A		A	T	E			V	I	O	L
A	Z	T	E	C		L	U	G		A	I	S	L	E
C	A	R	E	T		E	G	G		D	A	L	E	S
E	L	A	N		F	U	S	S	E	D		E	O	S
R	E	P		W	E	T		H	A	U	L			
	A	S	S	E	T			E	S	P	O	U	S	E
			U	S	A		O	L	E		T	R	I	G
P	R	I	N	T		E	L	L		P	I	N	T	O
H	Y	M	N		E	N	D		C	O	O			
D	E	P	E	N	D	S			H	U	N	C	H	
			D	E	A	L		D	I	T		H	I	M
H	A	M		A	M	A	Z	O	N		P	A	P	A
A	L	O	F	T		V	E	T		C	A	R	P	S
J	O	N	A	H		E	R	E		D	I	G	I	T
J	E	T	S			S	O	D		T	R	E	E	S

Made in the USA
Lexington, KY
02 December 2019

58036102R00033